Focus on the SEASONS

Focus on
SPRING

By Rosie Seaman

Fearon Teacher Aids
Simon & Schuster Supplementary Education Group

ABOUT THE AUTHOR

Rosie Seaman is an educator, author, and television producer. She has written several books for children and her work has been highlighted in a number of national magazines. As director of children's programming for WKRG-TV in Mobile, Alabama, Ms. Seaman has developed a variety of educational programs for young children.

Ms. Seaman received her certification in the Montessori method of preschool education and bases her work on the Montessori philosophy that young children learn best through techniques that encourage manipulation, experimentation, and discovery of the world around them.

Editorial Director: Virginia L. Murphy

Editors: Marilyn Trow and Sue Mogard

Copyeditor: Lisa Schwimmer

Design: Terry McGrath

Production: Rebecca Speakes

Cover Design: Lucyna Green

Cover and Inside Illustration: Marilynn Barr

ISBN 0-86653-974-3

Contents

A Note from the Author

The *Focus on the Seasons* series teaches basic skills, concepts, and subject matter to young children through active participation and discovery. Arranged in four seasonal books, the activities offer young learners the opportunity to express themselves freely throughout the school year as they contribute to their school environment.

Focus on Spring helps children discover some of the changes of this fascinating season. Children explore nature using their senses, learn about animals, enjoy spring through art, and celebrate spring with their families.

Invite the children to help set up an area in the classroom for sharing completed projects about spring. For example, a specific wall space and table may be used to display the children's creations. Displaying children's work is important to reinforce visually the skills and concepts they learn each day.

Use this book as a way of opening many other exciting avenues for exploring spring with the children. The results will be an accumulation of endless treasures that will always be of great value to both you and your young students. Have fun together!

Rosie Seaman

Introduction

The *Focus on the Seasons* series encourages you, the teacher, to be actively involved with the children and their learning. Each seasonal book provides children with an opportunity to learn about the seasons, as well as one another, through hands-on experiences with a variety of materials.

The format of each book offers easy reference to activities that explore commonly used early-childhood units, as well as suggesting a hands-on approach for implementing the activities into existing programs. Each book presents simple directions and bold illustrations and includes a bibliography of quality children's books to enhance the seasonal themes.

The activities begin with a list of materials to gather and offer suggested discussion questions. Each activity provides a step-by-step process for involving the children and suggests other alternatives when appropriate.

A SUGGESTED APPROACH

Prior to each activity:

➤ invite the children into the activity with the discussion questions, expanding the ideas presented in the questions as the children show interest.

➤ display the suggested materials on a low table in a work area that encourages the children to work independently.

During each activity:

➤ encourage the children to express their unique ideas through the materials.

➤ become involved with the children through conversations or mutual participation in the projects.

Following each activity:

➤ place the materials in a learning center in the classroom for the children to explore during independent time.

➤ display the children's completed creations in the classroom for you and the children to enjoy.

OBSERVING THE CHANGES OF SPRING

SPRING is a season filled with many changes. Through hands-on activities, the children will discover some signs of spring, the unique weather patterns of spring, and how spring differs from winter.

A Spring Stroll

MATERIALS

➤ a long sheet of butcher paper (print "Signs of Spring" in large letters across the top)

➤ marking pens or crayons

➤ jacket, raincoat, umbrella, and other appropriate spring clothing and items

SHARING TOGETHER

➤ What kind of clothing do you wear outdoors on a spring day? Hold up the different spring clothing and items for the children to observe or study. Invite different children to hold an umbrella and model a jacket, raincoat, and other appropriate springtime clothing.

➤ What do you think you might see on a walk outdoors that tells you that spring is coming? What do you think you might hear? Does spring bring special smells? What kinds of smells tell you spring is here? Name some spring items you can touch on a walk.

➤ Do you think spring is a special season? What makes spring a special season? What do you like best about spring?

WORKING TOGETHER

Invite the children to wear appropriate clothing on a designated day for a spring walk outdoors. Be sure to obtain signed field-trip permission slips from the children's parents. Before the walk, discuss the need to be prepared for changeable spring weather. Enjoy a spring walk with the children, stopping once in a while to notice the sounds, smells, and sights of spring. Take the walk after a spring shower, if possible. Encourage the children to listen to the water dripping from trees, flowers, drains, and so on. Have the children smell the fresh air and water after the rain and look closely for water on the flowers and puddles on the sidewalks as well.

When you return to the classroom, ask the children to draw pictures about the spring walk on a long sheet of butcher paper spread across the floor. Some children may wish to dictate sentences about their drawings as well. Use the spring mural as a background for a bulletin-board display on spring in the classroom.

Let's Take a Vacation

MATERIALS

➤ suitcase

➤ objects for a car trip, such as clothing, an umbrella, toiletries, books, toys, a map, snacks, and so on

➤ objects you would *not* take on a car trip, such as a cake mixer, pots and pans, and so on

SHARING TOGETHER

➤ Explain to the children that some people like to take trips in the spring after the long winter. If you were planning a trip or vacation, where would you go? (You may need to explain what a vacation is to the children.) Would you take a trip in a car? What sounds does a car make? In a plane? Let me see you pretend to be a plane flying in the sky. On a train? What sounds does a train make? Let's get in a line and pretend to be a train.

➤ Are you going to a warm place on your trip or a cold place? What would you pack in your suitcase for your trip? Would you pack a heavy winter coat if you were going to a warm place? How about ice skates?

➤ What safety tips should you keep in mind on your trip? How can you stay safe in a car? How can you stay safe walking across the street?

WORKING TOGETHER

Use different items from home as well as items from the classroom for this activity. Spread all the items out on a table in front of you. Then say to the children, "Let's pretend we are going on a car trip. What do you think we should pack in our suitcases?" Hold the items up, one at a time, and ask the children if you should pack each one.

After packing the suitcase with the help of the children, discuss some of the important safety rules they need to remember when taking a vacation.

Mirror Me

MATERIALS

➤ a full-length mirror

SHARING TOGETHER

➤ Have children look at themselves in a full-length mirror. What do you see in the mirror? Do you look different now than you did in the winter? How? Are you wearing different clothing? Is your hair shorter or longer? Trees, flowers, and animals sometimes change in the spring. How? Do people change in the spring? How?

➤ Have you ever played follow-the-leader? Do you know how to follow directions? (Play a modified follow-the-leader game, asking the children to raise their arms in the air, stand up and turn around, jump in place, and so on.)

WORKING TOGETHER

Invite the children to play a mirror game. Show the children a full-length mirror and discuss with the children what they see when they look in the mirror. Then explain to the children that they can be mirrors of each other. Ask two students to help you demonstrate this activity. Do this activity outside on a warm day.

Divide the class into pairs. Have each pair of students face one another. Ask one child in each pair to mirror the other child's actions. For example, if one child touches the left leg with his or her left hand, the other child should touch the right leg with his or her right hand. Invite one child in each pair to do three movements while the other child mirrors the action. Then ask the partners to switch and give the other child in each pair a chance to be the leader.

Signs That Signal

MATERIALS

➤ safety signs, such as a stop sign, stoplight, "beware of dog" sign, and so on (you can buy signs at a hardware store or make your own)

➤ marking pens or crayons

➤ construction paper

➤ scissors

➤ white paper

SHARING TOGETHER

➤ Do you have safety signs in your neighborhood? Which ones? Can you name some safety signs that you see when you are in a car? What do the signs mean? What color is a stop sign? What do you do when you see a stop sign? Do you know what colors are on a stoplight? (Show the children a picture of a stoplight.) What does a green light mean on a stoplight?

➤ What other safety signs do you know? Why do you think we have safety signs? Let's talk about other things that keep us safe. Should you cross the street by yourself? What should you do when you cross the street?

WORKING TOGETHER

Tape several safety signs to the bulletin board or on a wall in the classroom. Ask the children if any of the signs are familiar. Discuss the meanings of the signs. If possible, take the children on a walk around the school neighborhood and ask them to notice the signs around them. Be sure to obtain signed field-trip permission slips from the children's parents. Help the children make a list of the signs that they see on the walk.

Point out all of the signs you see to the children. Seeing the safety signs again and again helps reinforce the children's learning of what the safety signs mean. Invite the children to watch what cars do when they come to a stop sign or stoplight. Review what the different colors mean on a stoplight as well.

Invite the children to draw a picture of their favorite safety sign. Or, suggest that they draw pictures of themselves crossing the street safely.

Make a Rainbow

MATERIALS

➤ red, orange, yellow, green, and blue colors of tissue paper (cut in small pieces)

➤ large sheets of white construction paper (draw a rainbow outline on each sheet)

➤ diluted glue

➤ paintbrushes

➤ marking pens or crayons (red, orange, yellow, green, and blue)

SHARING TOGETHER

➤ Show the children a picture of a rainbow. What is this a picture of? Have you ever seen a real rainbow? When? Where? What colors do you see in a rainbow?

➤ Why does it rain so much in the spring? Did you know that plants and flowers need water to grow? Do you think people need water to grow, too? They do. Everything that grows needs water—even people!

WORKING TOGETHER

Invite the children to make rainbows. Show the children a picture of a rainbow. Then give each child a large sheet of white construction paper with a rainbow outline. Help the children spread glue on their rainbow outlines with paintbrushes. Encourage the children to arrange different colors of tissue-paper pieces on the rainbow outlines. Display the completed rainbows on a Sharing Wall in the classroom as reminders of the changing weather of spring.

What Does a Seed Need?

MATERIALS

➤ fast-growing flower seeds, such as pansies or marigolds

➤ potting soil

➤ plastic-coated paper cups or small flowerpots

➤ water

SHARING TOGETHER

➤ Have you ever planted a seed? What did it grow into? When do you plant seeds? Do you plant seeds in the winter? Why do you think you plant seeds in the spring?

➤ Do you know what a seed needs to grow? Seeds need air, water, and light. Do you know how to take care of a growing flower or plant? How?

WORKING TOGETHER

Invite the children to plant their own flowers. Fill several cups or small flowerpots with potting soil. Help the children plant seeds in their flowerpots. Explain to the children that seeds need air, water, and light to grow. Place the pots on a windowsill or another well-lighted area. Remind the children that they need to check their flowerpots every day to see if the soil needs water. Explain that they must not overwater the soil or the seeds will die. Check the pots daily as a class and show the children how to care for their growing seeds. Invite the children to take their plants home once they have bloomed.

Straw-Blowing

MATERIALS

➤ straws

➤ tempera paint

➤ large sheets of white paper

TEMPERA PAINT
RED

SHARING TOGETHER

➤ What makes clouds move in the sky? Pretend to be the wind and blow clouds across the sky. Now pretend to be a cloud blowing in the wind. Do clouds move fast or slow?

WORKING TOGETHER

Give each child a sheet of white paper and a straw. Drop small amounts of tempera paint in the center of each child's paper. Invite the children to use straws to pretend to be the wind and gently blow the tempera paint in many different directions across their papers.

Encourage the children to discuss the various shapes in each picture and then use their imaginations to suggest what the different shapes look like. Display the blow-art pictures on a Sharing Wall in the classroom.

Water-Puddle Game

MATERIALS

➤ blue poster paper
(cut in the shapes
of water puddles)

SHARING TOGETHER

➤ Point out that it often rains in the spring. What do you wear outside when it rains? Why do you sometimes wear boots in the spring?

WORKING TOGETHER

Invite the children to help make a water-puddle obstacle course in the classroom by placing several blue poster-paper puddles on the floor. Encourage the children to jump over the paper puddles to keep from getting their feet "wet" as they go through the spring obstacle course, first on one foot, then with both feet, and finally by alternating feet. Have adult volunteers on hand to "spot" the children as they go through the obstacle course. Join the children in cheering for their classmates each time they get through the obstacle course without touching the puddles!

Spring Pictures

MATERIALS

➤ white construction paper

➤ marking pens or crayons

➤ winter picture

SHARING TOGETHER

➤ Look outside the classroom window. Have the trees changed since winter? How? How has the playground changed since winter?

➤ What do you see outside in the spring that you don't see outside in the winter? What happens to snow in the spring? Is it still cold outside in the spring? What animals can you see outside in the spring?

WORKING TOGETHER

Invite the children to look closely at a winter picture and then discuss how various parts of the picture would probably change as spring approaches. Will the trees look different? How? Will there be more animals outside? Why?

After the discussion, give each child a sheet of construction paper and ask him or her to use marking pens or crayons to draw spring pictures showing the many changes outdoors since winter.

LEARNING ABOUT ANIMALS

IN THE SPRING, many baby animals are born. Through these activities, children learn about animals, their physical appearances, their movements, and their unique sounds.

Bunny Hop

MATERIALS

➤ pink paper plates

➤ long, pink balloons

➤ ribbon or string

➤ stapler (adult use only)

➤ hole punch

➤ music

SHARING TOGETHER

➤ Did you know that many baby animals are born in the spring? Let's name some animals that are born in the spring.

➤ Let's describe what a rabbit looks like. Where do rabbits live? What do they eat? What do you call a baby rabbit? How do bunnies move?

WORKING TOGETHER

Invite the children to make bunny hats for a bunny hop parade. Help each child carefully blow up two pink balloons. Tie the ends of the two balloons and then staple the balloon ends to the side rims of a paper plate for ears. Punch a hole on either side of the paper plates. Show the children how to make large knots at the ends of 8" to 10" pieces of ribbon or string and thread the ribbons or strings through each hole so that the children may tie their bunny hats under their chins. Play music and join the children in the bunny hop!

Animal Number Puzzles

MATERIALS

➤ pictures of animals cut from magazines (or you may want to draw several pictures of animals)

➤ large index cards

➤ marking pens

SHARING TOGETHER

➤ How high can you count? Let's count to five. Let's count to ten. Can you count higher? Who can count to fifteen? Let's try it.

➤ Did you know that some animals have more than one baby at a time? Can you name some animals that have lots of babies at once (dogs, cats, chickens, and so on)?

WORKING TOGETHER

Before beginning this activity, draw a zigzag line in the middle of several large index cards with a black marking pen. Draw a number on one side of the zigzag and glue or draw the appropriate number of animal pictures on the other side, such as 1 horse, 2 deer, 3 chicks, 4 puppies, and so on. Then cut along the zigzag to separate the numbers from the animals.

Spread the puzzle pieces on a table with the number pieces on one side of the table and the picture pieces on the other. Invite the children to put together the puzzle cards by matching the number cards with the corresponding picture cards. You may also reverse the matching process and invite the children to match the picture cards with the corresponding number cards. Use the puzzles as counting flashcards throughout the year.

Animal Cookie Fun

MATERIALS

➤ pictures of
   animals with
   whiskers, such as
   cats, dogs, lions,
   and so on

➤ animal cookies

➤ peanut butter

➤ butter knives

➤ napkins

SHARING TOGETHER

➤ Why do you think we see more animals in the spring than we do in the winter? (Discuss hibernation with the children.) Let's make a list of all the animals you can think of that we see in the spring.

➤ Can you name an animal that has horns? Can you name an animal that has a pink nose? What are whiskers? Did you know that animals with whiskers use the whiskers to feel? Do all animals have whiskers? Which animals have whiskers? (Show the children pictures of animals with whiskers.)

➤ What animals live in the forest? What animals live in the jungle? Have you ever been to the zoo? What animals have you seen there?

WORKING TOGETHER

Ask the children to wash their hands and help you wash the surface of a work table. Place animal cookies on the clean surface. Invite the children to find matching animal cookies. Then help the children put the cookies together by spreading one cookie with peanut butter and placing the matching cookie on top. Encourage the children to take turns describing the animals they match to the rest of the class. Then enjoy eating the animal treats together!

Alligator!

MATERIALS

➤ picture of an alligator

➤ green construction paper

➤ beads, sequins, or colored buttons

➤ scissors

➤ glue

➤ clothespins

SHARING TOGETHER

➤ Show the children a picture of an alligator. Can you describe what an alligator looks like? Have you ever seen a real alligator? Where? Have you ever seen a baby alligator?

➤ Show the children a picture of an alligator. What kind of an animal is an alligator? Where does an alligator live? Do you know that alligators usually live in warm places? What does an alligator eat? Do you think an alligator's skin is rough or smooth?

WORKING TOGETHER

Before beginning this activity, read aloud a fiction or nonfiction book on alligators, if possible. Then invite the children to make paper alligators. Cut pieces of construction paper into strips. Show the children how to make loop chains with the strips until each child's loop chain is about a foot long. Clip a clothespin to one end of the loop chain for the alligator's mouth. Invite the children to glue beads, sequins, or buttons on either side of the clothespins for eyes. Display the alligators in the classroom or encourage the children to take their alligators home to show their families!

Animal Masks

MATERIALS

➤ pictures of various animals

➤ paper plates (cut eye holes in each plate for the children)

➤ constuction paper in various colors

➤ marking pens or crayons

➤ glue

➤ yarn

➤ scissors

➤ popsicle sticks

SHARING TOGETHER

➤ Can you name some animals you might see outside in the spring? Why might you see more animals outside in the spring than in the winter? What keeps animals warm in the winter? Do you know that an animal's fur is sometimes called a coat? Animals shed some of their winter fur in the spring, just like we take off our coats when we come indoors where it is warm. Why do we do that?

➤ Can you act like an animal? Which animal are you? Let's pretend we are animals. Pick an animal you'd like to be. Can you make sounds like your animal? Let's try it together.

WORKING TOGETHER

Invite the children to make animal masks. Encourage the children to draw animal faces on paper plates using marking pens or crayons. Help the children cut ears from construction paper to glue on the animal masks. Then have the children cut strips of yarn to glue on the masks for hair, if desired. Glue a popsicle stick to the bottom of each mask.

Suggest that the children use the animal masks as they act out some animal sounds and movements. Encourage the rest of the class to guess the animal pantomimed.

Fish Mural

MATERIALS

➤ pictures of a shark and a goldfish (as well as other fish, if you wish)

➤ mural-size sheet of butcher paper

➤ newspaper

➤ blue fingerpaint

➤ sand

➤ several pre-cut fish (cut from construction paper in a variety of sizes and colors)

➤ small bowls or cups

SHARING TOGETHER

➤ Have you ever been fishing? Have you ever been to a lake or to the ocean? Have you seen fish there? What kinds of fish? Were the fish big or little?

➤ Show the children a picture of a shark and a picture of a goldfish. Here are two fish. Which fish is big? Which fish is little? Can you point to the big fish? What is the big fish called? This is a shark. Sharks swim in the ocean. Can you point to the little fish? What is this fish called? This is a goldfish. Goldfish swim in lakes and streams. Do any of you have a goldfish as a pet? Tell us about your goldfish.

WORKING TOGETHER

Invite the children to make a fish mural. Cover the floor with newspaper and place a mural-size sheet of butcher paper on top. Place small bowls or cups of fingerpaint on the newspapers and invite the children to gather around the paper. Remind the children to wear paint shirts or smocks. Invite the children to make waves with the fingerpaint on the butcher paper. Encourage children to cover the entire sheet of paper. Then help the children wash their hands.

Ask the children if they know what is under the water in a lake or in the ocean. Then encourage the children to sprinkle sand at the bottom edge of the butcher paper to make the ocean or lake floor. Give each child several small paper fish and ask them to put the fish in the water by sticking them to the fingerpaint. Display the mural in the classroom or use the mural as a background for a bulletin-board display.

Stand-Up Animal Snacks

MATERIALS

- pictures of a variety of animals, including a giraffe
- animal-shape cookie cutters
- peanut butter
- butter knives
- bread

SHARING TOGETHER

➤ Let's list as many animals as we can think of. What sound does each animal make? Which animals roar? Which animals make quiet sounds? Which animals make loud sounds? Do you know any animals that make funny sounds?

➤ Do you know any animals that make hardly any sound at all? (Show the children a picture of a giraffe.) Do you know that giraffes are very quiet animals? Let's pretend to be giraffes quietly eating leaves from the trees.

WORKING TOGETHER

Invite the children to make their own animal snacks. Show the children how to use animal-shape cookie cutters to cut out two identical animal shapes from slices of bread. Help the children spread peanut butter on the cut bread shapes and place the shapes together to make special animal sandwiches! Ask the children to act out the animals for the others to guess. Encourage the children to walk and make sounds with their animal snacks. Then invite the children to eat their snacks!

Egg Carton Turtles

MATERIALS

➤ pictures of turtles

➤ green construction paper

➤ cardboard egg cartons

➤ glue

➤ marking pens or crayons

SHARING TOGETHER

➤ Can you describe a turtle? Is a turtle's shell hard or soft? Where do turtles live? What do they eat? Do you know that some large turtles live to be more than one hundred years old? Some even live to be 120! Would you like to live to be 120?

➤ Have you ever had a turtle as a pet? Tell us about your turtle. What do you feed your turtle? How old is your turtle?

WORKING TOGETHER

Before beginning this activity, cut green construction paper into turtle shapes and cut the egg cartons into twelve separate egg sections. Read a fiction or nonfiction book on turtles to the children before the activity, if possible.

Invite the children to make egg carton turtles. Give each child a green construction-paper turtle shape and one egg section. Invite the children to color the egg sections with crayons or marking pens in a turtle-shell design. Help the children glue the egg sections, open end down, on the construction-paper turtle shapes to make the turtle's shell. Encourage the children to draw in the turtle's eyes, nose, and mouth.

EXPLORING SPRING THROUGH MY SENSES

ENCOURAGING children to use their senses helps them uncover rich information about the spring season. These activities invite the children to use their senses to explore springtime foods, textures of things found outdoors in the spring, how spring sounds are made, and sharpens their senses of sight and hearing.

Make an Impression

MATERIALS

➤ items that are rough and items that are smooth, such as a cheese grater, a piece of plastic, sandpaper, felt, and so on

➤ drawing paper

➤ paperless crayons

SHARING TOGETHER

➤ Can you name some things found outdoors in the spring that feel rough? Can you name some things found outdoors in the spring that feel smooth? What are some things found outdoors in the spring that are soft?

➤ Show the children things with different textures, such as the rough and smooth items listed under materials. What do you think this is (hold up a cheese grater)? Do you think it is rough or smooth? Let's feel it carefully. What is this (hold up a piece of sandpaper)? Do you think it is smooth or rough? Let's feel this, too. (Continue with other items, if you wish.)

WORKING TOGETHER

Invite the children to join you on a walk to discover things in nature that have interesting textures. Be sure to obtain signed field-trip permission slips from the children's parents. Show the children how to make rubbings of the items they find, such as tree bark, sticks, leaves, and so on. Place sheets of drawing paper over the items and then rub paperless crayons gently over the papers to reveal the interesting textures. Have the children share their texture rubbings with one another when they return to the classroom. Encourage the children to describe their drawings to the class.

If a walk isn't possible, you might invite the children to make rubbings of a sidewalk, the school building, or playground equipment to reveal unique textures.

Play a Tune

MATERIALS

➤ 8 water glasses
➤ water
➤ metal spoon

SHARING TOGETHER

➤ Close your eyes and listen. What sounds do you hear? Let's name some springtime sounds. Which sound is your favorite? What sounds do birds make? Do you think birds sound like music? How?

➤ Gently touch your throat while you say your name. Feel the vibration of your vocal cords as you speak. Put your hand over your mouth and say "hello." Let's do this together. Now take your hand away from your mouth and shout "hello." Let's do this together. Which is louder?

WORKING TOGETHER

Invite the children to do a sound experiment. Help the children fill eight water glasses with different amounts of water. Encourage the children to line up the glasses in order from the least full to the most full. Then invite the children to take turns gently tapping the sides of the glasses with a metal spoon to hear the different sounds. Invite the children to play simple tunes by gently tapping the water glasses.

Fruit and Vegetable Guessing Game

MATERIALS

➤ large cardboard box with removeable top

➤ a variety of fruits and vegetables

➤ pictures of fruits and vegetables

SHARING TOGETHER

➤ Let's name some fruits. Let's name some vegetables. Where do fruits and vegetables come from? (Hold up pictures of a variety of fruits and vegetables.) What is this vegetable (or fruit)? Have you ever eaten this vegetable (or fruit) before? Did you like it? What does it taste like?

➤ What is your favorite fruit? What is your favorite vegetable? What color is your favorite fruit? What color is your favorite vegetable?

WORKING TOGETHER

Invite the children to play a fruit and vegetable guessing game. Cut two round holes on each side of a large cardboard box. Make the holes large enough for children to fit their hands through. Glue pictures of fruits and vegetables on the box. Place a variety of fruits and vegetables inside the box, one at a time to begin with, then increase the number and variety as children become better at guessing the contents.

Invite each child to reach through the holes to feel the fruit or vegetable inside the box. Give each child a moment to feel the fruit or vegetable completely. Then ask the child to guess the name of the fruit or vegetable and say the name aloud. Lift the top of the box to see if the child is correct. If so, encourage the child who guessed correctly to pass the fruit or vegetable around for others to feel and smell. After the activity, wash the fruits and vegetables thoroughly and then cut the fruits and vegetables up into small pieces and invite the children to taste them.

Musical Chairs

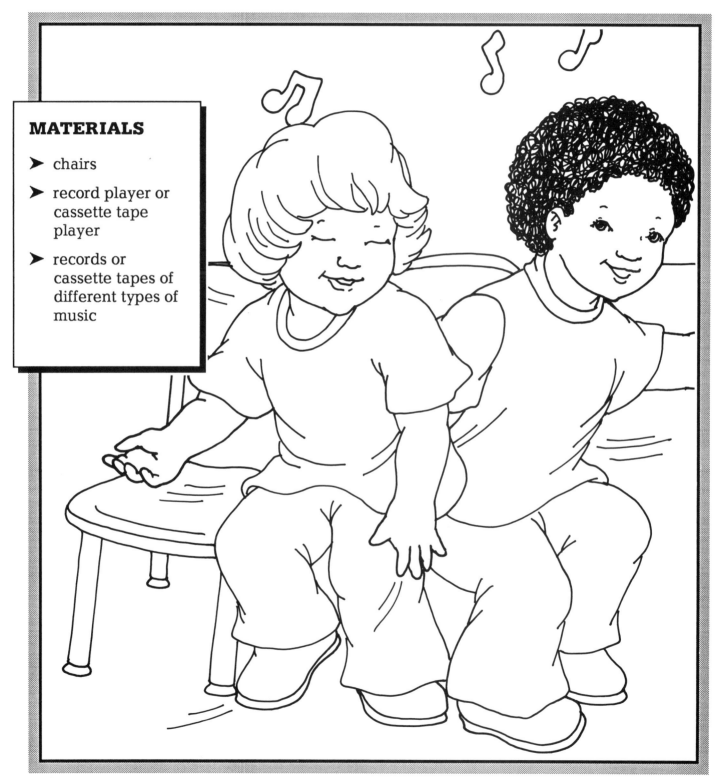

MATERIALS

➤ chairs

➤ record player or cassette tape player

➤ records or cassette tapes of different types of music

SHARING TOGETHER

➤ Let's pretend we are birds and make bird sounds together. Do you know that each kind of bird makes a special sound? Sometime when you are outside, listen to the different sounds the different birds make.

➤ Listen as I play some music. Does the sound of the music make you feel like moving? Can you move in time to the music? Move in a new way when I change the music.

WORKING TOGETHER

Play musical chairs. This is a great activity to help children release some energy. Encourage laughter and fun as the children use their listening powers to play the game. Have the children march around a circle of chairs as you play some music. Explain to the children that each time the music stops, they should quickly sit down on the chairs nearest to them. When the music begins again, one chair will be removed. Tell the children that each time you start and stop the music, another chair will be taken away. Invite the children who are left standing without chairs each time to work independently in learning centers. Continue until all of the children have left the circle.

Pass It On

MATERIALS

➤ none

SHARING TOGETHER

➤ What sounds do you hear in the spring that you might not hear in the winter? Let's pretend we are spring animals or insects. What animal or insect are you? Can you make the sounds that your animal or insect makes? Let's try it together.

➤ What part of your body do you use to listen? How do you tell a friend a secret (whisper in their ear)? Do you talk loudly or softly when you whisper? Show me how you whisper to a friend.

WORKING TOGETHER

Invite the children to sit together with you in a circle on the floor in a large, carpeted area. Explain that you will whisper a sentence about spring to the child sitting next to you. Ask that child to whisper the same sentence to the next child, repeating it as best as he or she remembers. Continue until the sentence reaches the last child in the circle. Invite that child to repeat the sentence aloud for the entire group. Help the children compare the sentence with the sentence you began with. Ask the children why they think the sentence is different. Continue the game with new sentences and new beginning points. Encourage the children to speak clearly and listen carefully when a message is being passed.

After the game, invite the children to go outside and practice listening very carefully to the sounds of spring. Make a list of the sounds the children hear. Encourage children to listen for and add new sounds to the list each day.

Look and Tell

MATERIALS

➤ magazine pictures of spring scenes (mount each picture on construction paper)

➤ stopwatch

SHARING TOGETHER

➤ Look at the child sitting next to you. Close your eyes and describe what he or she is wearing. Try to remember everything you can about his or her clothing. Can you remember the colors?

➤ Can you describe how the playground looks without looking at it? Now look outside and see how much you were able to remember.

WORKING TOGETHER

Invite the children to look carefully at a spring picture for 30 seconds, using a stopwatch to keep track of the time. Then ask children to describe the picture after you have taken it away from view. Encourage the children to look at the picture once again and discuss the details that were not remembered. Repeat the game using different spring scenes.

Painting with Pudding

MATERIALS

➤ canned or
  pre-packaged,
  prepared vanilla
  pudding

➤ wax paper or
  high-gloss
  wrapping paper

➤ food coloring

SHARING TOGETHER

➤ What do you see outside that lets you know that spring is here? What kinds of animals do you see in the spring? What kinds of plants? How does the sky look? How does the ground look?

➤ What can you do outside in the spring? Can you have a snowball fight in the spring? Can you sled down a hill in the spring? What games do you play outside in the spring?

WORKING TOGETHER

Invite the children to make spring paintings with pudding! Place newspaper on a large table. Ask the children to gather around the table. Encourage the children to wear smocks or paint shirts for this activity.

Give each child a sheet of wax paper or high-gloss wrapping paper. Place a large spoonful of the prepared pudding on each child's sheet of paper. Add a couple drops of food coloring to each child's pudding. Ask the child what color they would like. Then invite the children to fingerpaint with the pudding. Ask children to fingerpaint spring objects, such as flowers, trees, animals, and so on. Encourage the children to use their imaginations.

Form a Shape

MATERIALS

➤ different geometric shapes, in various sizes and colors, cut from construction paper

SHARING TOGETHER

➤ Show me a circle. Can you name some things outside that are shaped like a circle? What are they? What are some things in the classroom that are shaped like a circle?

➤ Can you name some things shaped like a circle on your body (head, eyes, navel)?

➤ Name something shaped like a rectangle on your body (foot).

WORKING TOGETHER

Invite the children to look carefully at different construction-paper shapes as you hold each shape up for the children to see. Identify each shape for the children. Ask the children if they can form their bodies into the different shapes shown.

Divide the class into small groups. Give each group a different construction-paper shape. Have the children work together in the groups to find items outside that match the different shapes. Then suggest that the children take turns pantomiming shapes and asking others to find shapes that match.

ENJOYING SPRING WITH MY FAMILY

THE FAMILY is an integral part of a child's world. In this section, children tell about their families and make special spring gifts to share with family members.

Fun with Mom and Dad

MATERIALS

➤ oranges

➤ large lettuce leaves

➤ raisins

➤ toothpicks

➤ cherries

➤ small paper plates

SHARING TOGETHER

➤ What are some things you enjoy doing with your parents? Is there a special place you go with your Dad? Tell us about it. Is there a special place you go with your Mom? Where? Share how you feel when you go different places with your parents, such as to the dentist or to a circus.

➤ Tell about something funny that happened when you were with your parents. You can tell us something sad if you want to, too.

WORKING TOGETHER

Invite the children to make special orange faces. Ask the children to wash their hands, then help you wash a working surface as well. Show the children how to arrange some large lettuce leaves on small paper plates and place an orange on top of each leaf. Help the children use toothpicks to attach raisins and cherries to the oranges to make faces. Encourage the children to make happy faces on one side of the oranges and sad or silly faces on the other.

Ask the children to hold up the appropriate sides of their oranges to show how they might feel if they were to go to some of the following places with their parents (read aloud each place):

circus	camp
sports game	swimming pool
the doctor	the dentist
restaurant	roller skating rink
school activity	lake

Talk about why some places make the children feel happy and some places make them feel sad. After the discussion, help the children remove the toothpicks from their oranges and enjoy the nutritious snacks with their friends.

Family Game

MATERIALS

➤ dolls

➤ dress-up clothes, hats, shoes

➤ books, purses, jackets, and other things the children can use to role-play families

➤ large cardboard boxes

SHARING TOGETHER

➤ How many people are in your family? Do you have any brothers and sisters? How many? Do you have fun with your brothers and sisters? What kinds of things do you do?

➤ Do you like to share? Do you share things with your parents? Do you share things with your brothers or sisters? What important rules do you have at home?

WORKING TOGETHER

Before beginning this activity, put the clothing in boxes, labeling each box appropriately, such as "hats," "coats," "shoes," and so on. Do the same with the props, such as "kitchen supplies," etc. Then divide the class into small groups. Invite the children to put on the costumes and pretend to be a parent, guardian, brother, sister, uncle, or any other member of a family. Provide props from home or use items from the classroom. Encourage the children to use their imaginations and role-play a family working together to make dinner, helping with the housework, taking a walk, and so on. Remind the children that they need to share all the chores, such as cooking, cleaning, taking care of the baby, and so on. After playing the game, remind the children to clean up by placing the items back in the correct boxes.

A Ring Holder for Mom, My Sister, or Grandma

MATERIALS

➤ empty spools
➤ short, unsharpened pencils
➤ yarn
➤ glue
➤ marking pens
➤ wrapping paper

SHARING TOGETHER

➤ Can you describe your mom, grandma, or sister? What does she like to do? What special spring things do you do with your mom, grandma, or sister? Do you play games? Do you garden? Do you take walks, go to the park, or go to the zoo?

➤ How do you tell your mom, grandma, or sister that you love her? Do you give her hugs and kisses? How about presents? What kinds of presents have you given your mom, grandma, or sister?

WORKING TOGETHER

Invite the children to each make a ring holder for mom, a sister, or grandma. Show the children how to glue a pencil into the hole in the middle of an empty spool. Help the children use yarn, glue, and marking pens to make faces of their moms, sisters, or grandmas on the spools. Encourage the children to be creative.

Ask the children to help you wrap the ring holders once the glue has dried. Encourage the children to give the ring holders to their mothers, sisters, or grandmas on Mother's Day.

A Bookmark for Dad, My Brother, or Grandpa

MATERIALS

➤ 12" lengths of wide ribbon

➤ gummed stickers

➤ marking pens or crayons

SHARING TOGETHER

➤ What special things do you do in the spring with your dad, grandpa, or brother? Do you play games? What kinds of games? Do you take walks or go to the zoo?

➤ What is your favorite story? Does somebody at home read to you? Who? Does your dad, grandpa, or brother like to read books?

WORKING TOGETHER

Invite the children to make bookmarks. Encourage children to decorate 12" lengths of wide ribbons with stickers and then use marking pens to draw other designs, if desired. Place the bookmarks in favorite books and give to dad, a brother, or grandpa.

EXPLORING SPRING THROUGH ART

ART is a fun, productive way of learning all about the spring season. Using different materials, the children can make tissue flowers, kites, and even have their own outdoor art exhibit.

Tissue-Tear Flowers

MATERIALS

- ➤ pictures of a variety of flowers
- ➤ several colors of tissue paper
- ➤ diluted glue
- ➤ paintbrushes
- ➤ construction paper
- ➤ marking pens and crayons

SHARING TOGETHER

➤ Can you name some flowers that you see in the spring? Can you describe a tulip? (Show the children a picture of a tulip.) Can you describe a rose? (Show the children a picture of a rose.) Do you know that roses have thorns? Look at this picture of a rose. Can you see the thorns on the stems? Can you point out the stem of the flower on this picture? (Show other pictures of flowers and continue the discussion of flowers with the children.)

➤ When do people give flowers? Do you know any holidays when people get flowers sent to them? Which ones? Are there other times people get flowers? When?

WORKING TOGETHER

Invite the children to make tissue-paper flowers. Show the children how to brush diluted glue on the center areas of sheets of construction paper. Have children arrange torn tissue-paper pieces on the glue in overlapping designs. After the glue is dry, invite the children to use marking pens or crayons to outline the designs. Children may wish to add stems and leaves to their tissue-paper designs. Display the tissue-paper flowers on a Sharing Wall or encourage the children to take their flower pictures home to share with their families.

Paper-Towel Painting

MATERIALS

➤ a picture of a rainbow

➤ tempera paints (red, orange, yellow, green, and blue)

➤ small box of crayons

➤ paper towels

➤ white construction paper

SHARING TOGETHER

➤ Show the children a picture of a rainbow. Do you know what this is? Do you know what causes a rainbow? Who has seen a rainbow? What colors do you see in a rainbow? (Show the children a small box of crayons.) Look at this box of crayons. Pick out the colors you see in a rainbow.

WORKING TOGETHER

Invite the children to create their own rainbows. Show the children how to dip wadded paper towels into the tempera paints and then use the towels to paint rainbows or other spring designs on sheets of white construction paper. Keep the picture of the rainbow in view for the children to use as a reference. Encourage the children to be creative with their colors. Ask the children to discard the paper towel "brushes" once the towels have become saturated. Display the special designs in the classroom on a Sharing Wall as reminders of spring.

Dip-and-Dye Kite Designs

MATERIALS

➤ tempera paints (red, orange, yellow, green, and blue)

➤ paper towels

➤ marking pens

➤ construction paper

➤ rope or clothesline

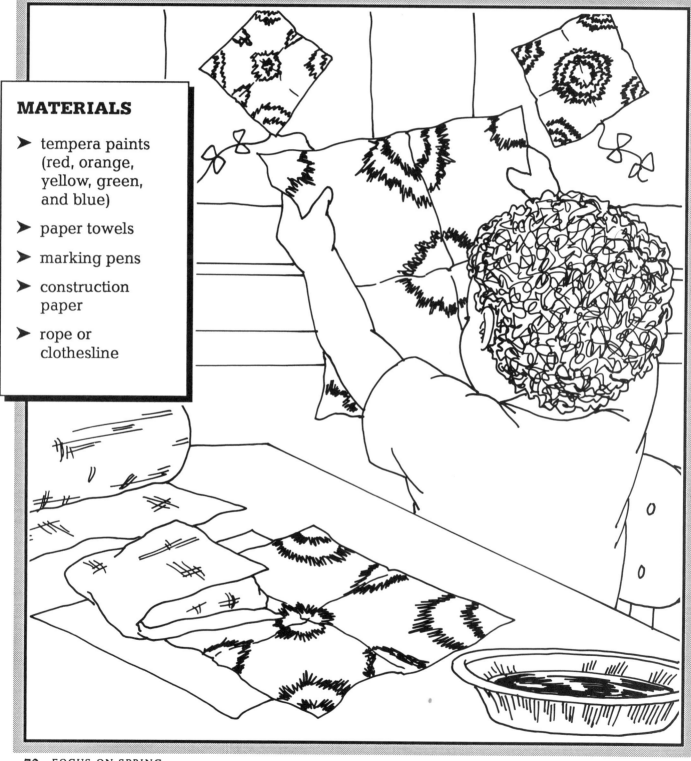

SHARING TOGETHER

➤ What colors remind you of spring? Why? Name some of the colors in a rainbow. What are some of the colors you see in the sky? What colors are the trees? Flowers? What are some of your favorite colors?

➤ What activity is fun to do on windy spring days? Have you ever flown a kite on a windy day? Tell us about it.

WORKING TOGETHER

Invite the children to make their own colorful kites. Give each child a paper towel. Invite the children to fold the paper towels in half twice to form squares. Then show children how to dip each corner of the folded paper-towel squares into different colors of paint. Open the towels to reveal unique tie-dye designs.

Hang the towels on a line to dry. Pin the tie-dye designs on a bulletin board and then show the children how to use marking pens or crayons to draw kite strings. Help the children cut kite tails from construction paper to pin on the kites as well.

Outdoor Art Exhibit

MATERIALS

➤ large cardboard boxes (1 for every 4 students)

➤ butcher paper (to fit each side of each box)

➤ tempera paints

➤ paintbrushes

➤ bowls

➤ water

SHARING TOGETHER

➤ Have you ever been to an art show or an art museum? What did you see there?

➤ What are some of the things that remind you of spring? Does snow remind you of spring? How about sleds? How about birds or flowers? Let's paint things that remind us of spring.

WORKING TOGETHER

Invite the children to sponsor their own outdoor art exhibit. Cover all sides of each of the boxes with butcher paper. Outside, on school grounds, or in a park (be sure to get parental permission if going to the park), set out bowls of tempera paint, paintbrushes, and water for the children's use. Divide the class into groups of four—one child for each side of the boxes. Encourage the children to paint their special side of the box in any way they would like. Help the children sign their creations.

Invite parents, grandparents, and other classes to an exhibition of the children's box art. Afterwards, use the boxes for storage in the classroom.

Eggshell Mosaic Mural

MATERIALS

➤ dyed eggshells
(ask the children
beforehand to
save any
eggshells from
home)

➤ glue

➤ butcher paper

SHARING TOGETHER

➤ What kinds of flowers do you see outside in the spring? Do you see animals? What kinds of animals? What does the sky look like in the spring? What do the trees look like?

➤ Have you ever seen a bird fly? How does it fly? Can you show me? Show me how a butterfly flies. Can you tell me what a butterfly looks like?

WORKING TOGETHER

Invite the children to make a springtime mural out of eggshells. Spread the materials listed on page 74 out on a table. As a class, plan with the children what kinds of things they will put in the mural, as well as where things might go. Include a garden path, trees, the sky, the ground, butterflies, birds, and so on. Divide the class into small groups. Assign each group to one part of the mural—one group can work on the sky, one group can make a garden, and so on. Younger children may wish to create one object for the mural, such as a bird, cloud, and so on. Help the children spread glue on the areas and then carefully sprinkle the eggshell pieces over the glue. (Use white eggshells for the garden path, if desired.) When the mosaic is dry, display the eggshell mosaic mural in the classroom.

Fruit-Print Garden

MATERIALS

➤ oranges and lemons

➤ small tray

➤ tempera paints

➤ paintbrushes

➤ flat dishes or pans

➤ butcher paper or construction paper

SHARING TOGETHER

➤ Have a tray of small lemon and orange pieces available for you and the children to taste. Keep these separate from the oranges and lemons you will be using for the activity. Do you eat oranges? What color is an orange? Do you eat lemons? What color is a lemon? Which tastes sweeter? Let's sample some. First, let's try the orange. Is it sweet or is it sour? Now let's try the lemon. Is it sweet or sour?

WORKING TOGETHER

Before beginning this activity, cut oranges and lemons in half and let them dry overnight. Put different colors of tempera paint in flat dishes or pans and place the pans on newspaper on the floor or on a work table in the classroom. Remind the children to put on paint shirts or smocks.

Give each child a sheet of butcher paper or construction paper. Invite the children to dip the fruit halves in the paints and then make a print on their papers. The fruits make a flower-like print on the paper. Encourage the children to make a fruit-print garden by adding stems, leaves, and so on.

Bibliography of Children's Books

Reading good books to children opens up worlds of information and stimulates imaginations! Establish an early love of reading in children by creating positive experiences with these seasonal selections. Use one or more of these books to introduce an activity, as a follow-up to an activity, or for individual use by the children during independent time.

BOOKS TO ENJOY DURING THE SPRING

Mr. Gumpy's Motor Car, John Burningham, Crowell, 1973.

Mushroom in the Rain, Mirra Ginsburg, Macmillan, 1974.

Planting a Rainbow, Lois Ehlert, Harcourt Brace Jovanovich, 1988.

Seasons, Heidi Goennel, Little, Brown and Company, 1986.

What Happens in the Spring, Kathleen Costello Beer, Books for Young Explorers, National Geographic Society, 1977.

A Year of Birds, Ashley Wolff, Dodd, Mead and Company, 1984.

OTHER BOOKS TO ENJOY THROUGHOUT THE YEAR

Annie and the Wild Animals, Jan Brett, Houghton Mifflin, 1985.

Calico Cat's Year, Donald Charles, Childrens Press, 1984.

First Comes Spring, Anne Rockwell, Crowell, 1985.

Frederick, Leo Lionni, Pantheon, 1967.

Growing Vegetable Soup, Lois Ehlert, Harcourt Brace Jovanovich, 1987.

Haircuts for the Woolseys, Tomie de Paola, Putnam Publishing Group, 1989.

The Little House, Virginia Lee Burton, Houghton Mifflin, 1942.

New Boots for Spring, Harriet Ziefert and Deborah Kogan Ray, Viking Press, 1989.

Ox-Cart Man, Donald Hall, Puffin Books, 1979.

Sunshine Makes the Seasons, Franklyn M. Branley, Crowell, 1974.

A Year in the Country, Douglas Florian, Greenwillow Books, 1989.